Cerebral Currency

Holistic Education & Human Capital Market

Emmanuel Ese

INTRODUCTION

"What do you want to be when you grow up?"

Most of us heard that question as kids. We answered with titles that sounded impressive. Doctor. Engineer. Scientist. Firefighter. Police officer. Then we got older, and life started editing our dreams. Not always because we lacked talent, but because we began to see how society really works and what it truly demands from us.

This book is written for young adults preparing to enter the workforce. I call this stage the human capital market. It is the part of life where your value is tested in real time. Not by your intentions, but by your skills, your discipline, your attitude, and your ability to deliver results.

Cerebral Currency is about mental wealth. It is the value you carry in your mind, your habits, and your character. It is what you can offer when nobody is coming to save you. If you already have the habit of reading, you have discovered one of the most powerful tools for self-leadership. Reading builds clarity. It expands perspective. It helps you think beyond your environment.

I started reading seriously in my twenties. It did not make my life perfect. Far from it. But it helped me avoid many mistakes that young adults commonly make. It also helped me set long term goals and stay consistent long enough to see real change.

I discovered the magic of reading around the age of twenty-two. During that period, I spent time with books that challenged how I thought and how I acted. Books like *The War of Art* by Steven Pressfield and *The Art of Thinking* by Ernest Dimnet. Those authors did not just teach ideas. They described the adult world with honesty. Through their experiences and reflections, I began to understand human nature and the hidden rules of progress.

Many people struggle because they are trained to believe that life must be a struggle. This belief is often inherited. Parents pass it to children. Communities repeat it until it becomes normal. Yes, life has challenges. Nobody escapes them. But your mindset decides whether challenges will shape you or break you.

As you step into the workforce, the world expects more from you. It expects accountability. It expects emotional control. It expects you to show up even when you do not feel ready. A large part of your success will depend on how well you handle responsibility.

The road is not easy. That is not meant to scare you. It is simply a reality that school rarely explains. But the good news is that you can reduce the difficulty by preparing yourself. You cannot rely only on formal education. There is a wider education available to you. Books, mentors, experience, and self-study can help you build the kind of intelligence that school does not test.

We no longer live in a world where conventional wisdom is enough. Your intellectual capital plays a major role in your opportunities, your productivity, and your confidence. One of the most reliable ways to increase your value is self-improvement through continuous learning. Sadly, many school systems rely on recycled curricula and outdated testing methods that do not fully prepare students for modern life.

This book also speaks about inner knowledge. Through neuroplasticity, you can train your mind, reshape your habits, and improve how you interact with the world. You can move from being reactive to being intentional. You can turn ideas into actions and actions into results.

I hope this book encourages you to practice what you learn and share what helps you. Knowledge alone is not power. Applied knowledge is power. You can know a lot and still stay stuck if you do not act on what you know.

YOUR DISCIPLINE

We all pass through an education system that tries to shape us into "useful" members of society. Every community has its own definition of success. That definition is repeated so often that it quietly becomes a script. From primary school to university, many of us start making career choices based on what we see around us, what people praise, and what our environment rewards.

This is why education matters. Not only because it gives knowledge, but because it trains the mind to think, to solve problems, and to make better decisions. Education can sharpen your intuition. It can also expand your view of what is possible beyond what you grew up seeing.

But here is the truth many young adults discover late. Formal education is only one part of the preparation. When you step into the workforce, you enter a different kind of classroom. That classroom tests your discipline in two ways. First, your competence. Second, your conduct.

This chapter is about both.

Discipline as a Field of Study

If you are currently in university, or you have just graduated, you have spent years learning a course. That course becomes your academic discipline because it is the area where you trained, where you gained technical knowledge, and where you earned a qualification that can open doors in the human capital market.

Choosing the right course matters. Most people eventually work in the field they studied, or in a closely related field. That is why your decision should not be based only on excitement, peer pressure, or family expectations. It should also be based on a realistic question.

Can I build a strong future with this path?

Some young adults know what they want early. Others discover it gradually. Both are normal. What matters is what you do after you choose. A degree alone is not a career. It is a starting signal.

I have met many students who think like this:
"I just need the certificate. Once I have it, I will get a good job."

I understand that mindset because I once carried it too. Sometimes, people get away with it because they have strong connections. Sometimes, they are simply lucky. But most people are not. For the majority, the job market does not reward wishes. It rewards value.

When an employer hires you, they are not paying for your effort. They are paying for your output. They are not investing in your dreams. They are investing in your skills.

This is why your academic discipline must become more than classroom knowledge. It must become competence. It must become the ability to deliver results under pressure, within deadlines, with consistency.

There are many qualified people in the job market. Many have degrees. Many have certificates. The difference is often not the paper. The difference is how prepared the person is.

Your goal should be to become the candidate who reduces stress for the organization, not the candidate who becomes extra work for everyone else. Proper preparation gives knowledge. Knowledge builds confidence. Confidence changes how you show up, speak, and perform.

In the human capital market, employers are not looking for how special you are to family and friends. They are looking for what is unique about your professional value.

Discipline as a Code of Behavior

Academic training may give you technical ability, but professional life also demands a code of behavior. Many young adults struggle in their first jobs, not because they lack intelligence, but because they struggle with workplace conduct.

The corporate world runs on structure. It runs on standards. It runs on boundaries. Even when the environment looks friendly, the expectations are still there.

Before you enter the job market, you should learn how to coexist professionally. You should learn how to communicate respectfully. You should learn how to manage yourself.

At work, you are no longer in your parents' home. You are no longer in your comfort zone. That requires awareness. It also requires humility.

If you make a mess in the coffee room, clean it. If you borrow something, return it. If you make a mistake, admit it early and correct it. These may sound small, but small behaviors become your reputation.

Do not expect the same patience that your friends and family give you. People who love you can tolerate your bad habits. Colleagues and managers evaluate performance. They also evaluate reliability.

In some workplaces, colleagues become friends. That can be a good thing. But it only works when you understand the difference between friendship and professional responsibility. Friendliness must not erase standards.

Many institutions offer internships to help students experience workplace settings. This is helpful, but internships do not always show the full reality of corporate life. Real work comes with pressure, consequences, and accountability.

Your discipline at work also includes respect for rules. It includes punctuality. It includes reading instructions. It includes understanding policies. It includes the simple habit of taking your job seriously.

Some people sign contracts without reading them. Later, they become shocked by expectations that were clearly written. Do not do that. Take time to read what you agree to. Ask questions when something is unclear. Being professional means, you pay attention.

Dress code also matters. Some industries are relaxed. Others are formal. Even when an industry is casual, your appearance still communicates something. It communicates attention to detail. It communicates self respect. It communicates judgement.

People expect doctors to look like doctors. They expect corporate managers to look like corporate managers. In many workplaces, how you present yourself influences how people trust you. If you manage money, people want to feel you are serious. If you represent an organization, your appearance becomes part of the brand.

Discipline also includes language. The workplace is not the street. There is a professional way to speak, even when you are angry. There is a professional way to disagree, even when you feel strongly. Choosing your words carefully is not weakness. It is self control.

Other forms of indiscipline include coming to work under the influence of substances, chronic lateness, absenteeism, sleeping on duty, harassment, and hostile behavior. These habits often begin long before the job. They become dangerous when they enter a professional environment.

A company pays you monthly for your contribution. That payment is an agreement. They meet financial obligations. You meet performance obligations. Professionalism means you honor your side.

Hard Skills and Soft Skills

Your discipline becomes stronger when you understand the two main pillars of workplace value: hard skills and soft skills.

Hard skills are technical abilities. They are learned through training. They are measurable through performance. They are often the reason you get invited for an interview.

Hard skills are your gateway into the human capital market. They are what you write on your CV to show that you can do the job.

But soft skills are what help you survive and grow once you enter.

Soft skills include communication, teamwork, emotional control, professionalism, reliability, problem solving, and work ethic. They are the skills that protect relationships in the workplace and help you work smoothly with people.

Modern employers increasingly value soft skills because technical ability alone is not enough in collaborative environments. A brilliant worker who creates conflict becomes a liability. A competent worker who communicates well becomes an asset.

Your growth in the workplace will often depend on how well you combine both disciplines. Academic discipline gives competence. Behavioral discipline builds trust.

Closing Thought

If you want to rise in the workplace, do not rely on magic. Build yourself deliberately. Prepare your hard skills. Train your soft skills. Practice professionalism until it becomes natural.

The human capital market rewards people who can deliver and behave like professionals while delivering.

If you can combine competence with good conduct, you will not only get opportunities. You will keep them.

YOUR PERSONALITY

Finding your place in the job market is one of the biggest decisions you will ever make. It shapes your income, your lifestyle, your confidence, and even the kind of people you spend time with. That is why you cannot treat career direction like a casual guess. Time moves fast, and while mistakes can be corrected, some mistakes are expensive in years, energy, and missed opportunities.

Personality matters because it affects how you work, how you communicate, and how you respond under pressure. Two people can have the same degree and still experience completely different results. One thrives because their nature fits the demands of the role. The other struggles, not because they are stupid, but because the environment keeps fighting their temperament.

This chapter will help you look inward and understand what makes you tick. Not so you can label yourself, but so you can manage yourself. Personality is not destiny. But personality is information, and information gives you power.

A Simple Temperament Framework

Many theories explain personality, but this book uses a simple temperament model that identifies four broad patterns:

Sanguine
Choleric
Melancholy
Phlegmatic

This model is not perfect, and you do not need to treat it like a strict rule book. Think of it as a mirror. Use the parts that help you and ignore what does not.

Most people are not just one temperament. Many of us are a blend. Still, there is often a dominant tendency that shows up in how we speak, work, and relate to others.

A note on temperament models, origin, and modern psychology

Before we go further, let us be clear about what this temperament framework is and what it is not.

The four temperament model, sanguine, choleric, melancholy, and phlegmatic, is one of the oldest personality lenses in recorded history. It is commonly linked to ancient Greek medicine and philosophy, especially the idea that human behavior was influenced by bodily fluids, often called the humors. Over time, the medical explanation faded, but the behavioral descriptions survived. They travelled across cultures, were repeated in religious and leadership writing, and eventually became popular in self development contexts because they feel intuitive and easy to remember.

However, in modern behavioral science, this model is considered **outdated and non standard**. Contemporary psychology does not use the four temperaments as a scientific framework for measuring personality, predicting behavior, or diagnosing traits. The medical roots behind it are not accepted, and the categories are too broad to capture the full complexity of human personality. In other words, the temperament model is not the tool that researchers use today when they want precision.

If you want a modern, research based model, the best starting point is the **Big Five** personality framework, often called OCEAN. It describes personality through five broad dimensions:

Openness to Experience
Conscientiousness
Extraversion
Agreeableness
Neuroticism

This model is widely used in contemporary research because it is measurable, testable, and better aligned with evidence based behavioral studies. It also avoids the problem of placing people into fixed labels. Instead, it describes personality on a spectrum, which is closer to how people actually function in real life.

So why mention the temperament model at all?

Because even when the science behind the original concept has been debunked, the descriptions can still feel strangely accurate. Not scientifically accurate in a lab sense, but psychologically familiar in a human sense. They describe patterns that many of us recognize in ourselves, our colleagues, and our families. They put messy human behavior into neat boxes, and that neatness can help a reader reflect quickly.

Think of it like this. The temperament model is not a microscope. It is a map. The map is not reality, but it can still help you navigate.

In this chapter, we will use temperament as a simple mirror for self awareness. If you recognize yourself in one of the descriptions, do not treat it as a final label. Treat it as a signal. Use it to identify strengths you can sharpen and weaknesses you can manage. Later, if you want deeper accuracy, you can explore the Big Five model and take a validated personality assessment.

For now, we will start with the old framework because it is relatable, easy to grasp, and surprisingly vivid at describing human nature.

Sanguine

A sanguine is often the person who brings energy into a room. They are naturally social, expressive, and upbeat. They can keep the atmosphere lively without even trying. In a professional setting, a well developed sanguine can be an excellent communicator, a strong presenter, and a natural organizer.

If your personality is sanguine, roles that involve people, interaction, events, communication, sales, marketing, customer relations, and team coordination may suit you, especially when you are disciplined.

But let us also be honest about the weak side.

An undeveloped sanguine can be noisy, restless, inconsistent, and too talkative. That restless energy can also lead to exaggeration because talking becomes a habit, not a choice. In serious environments, that can damage your credibility.

If you are sanguine, your growth depends on self control. You do not need to lose your brightness. You just need to learn when to switch it on and when to switch it off.

Choleric

A choleric is driven. They are bold, direct, goal focused, and often comfortable taking charge. They can make decisions quickly and push forward even when others hesitate. In the workplace, cholerics often perform well in leadership, strategy, project management, and high pressure roles where speed and decisiveness matter.

A choleric can be an asset because they move things forward. They do not like excuses. They like progress.

But the same traits can create trouble when they are not managed.

An untamed choleric can be aggressive, impatient, harsh, and emotionally explosive. They may treat people like tools. They may forget that human beings are not machines and that relationships are part of performance.

If you are choleric, your mission is not to become softer. Your mission is to become wiser. You can be strong without being cruel. You can be ambitious without being unbearable.

Be the leader people respect, not the leader people fear. In modern professional life, emotional intelligence is not optional. It is a career skill.

Melancholy

The melancholy temperament is often introspective, thoughtful, and deeply connected to creativity. Many melancholics are naturally analytical. Their minds can explore ideas in a powerful way. When they are well developed, they can become excellent writers, designers, researchers, strategists, innovators, and problem solvers.

A well groomed melancholy can build extraordinary things because they think beyond the obvious. They notice details others ignore. They care about meaning, quality, and purpose.

But the same intensity can become a burden.

An undeveloped melancholy may struggle with mood shifts, pessimism, overthinking, anxiety, and self sabotage. They may delay action because they want perfection. They may live too much in their mind and not enough in execution.

If you are melancholy, the key is balance. Your mind is a gift, but you must learn to manage it. Creativity is powerful, but it requires structure to become a career advantage.

Phlegmatic

The phlegmatic temperament is calm, steady, and peace oriented. Phlegmatics often know how to maintain professionalism and coexist with others without unnecessary conflict. They can be dependable team members because they do not always chase drama.

In the workplace, phlegmatics can do well in roles that require stability, long term consistency, administrative coordination, support functions, and patient leadership. Many phlegmatics are good listeners, and listening is a rare strength in corporate environments.

But the weak side can show up as passivity.

An undeveloped phlegmatic may procrastinate, avoid challenges, or settle for comfort. They may accept situations they should confront. They may resist growth because growth can feel stressful.

If you are phlegmatic, your mission is not to become loud. Your mission is to become intentional. You can keep your calm and still develop ambition.

Temperament is a Tool, Not a Prison

You can be a blend of temperaments. You can carry traits from your parents and still develop your own nature. The point of this chapter is not to put you in a box. The point is to help you understand yourself so you can improve.

If you are too playful without discipline, life will treat you as unserious.
If you are too harsh, people may avoid you.
If you are too sensitive without structure, you may struggle under pressure.
If you are too passive, you may watch opportunities pass you by.

The goal is growth.

When you understand your strengths, you can choose environments where those strengths are rewarded. When you understand your weaknesses, you can train yourself before the job market trains you through pain.

Closing Thought

Your personality influences your career, but it does not control your destiny. You can refine your temperament through self awareness, discipline, and consistent character work. That is the difference between raw potential and professional value.

APPRENTICESHIP

According to dictionary.com, an apprentice is a person who works for another to learn a trade. Apprenticeship is therefore a practical method of learning that can take a few months or several years, depending on the skill and the level of mastery required.

Yet apprenticeship does not enjoy the same prestige as formal education. In many societies, academic qualifications are praised more loudly than hands on competence. People celebrate certificates, but often ignore the quiet engine that keeps commerce alive: the passing down of usable skills from one person to another. Education can shape thinking and improve social behaviour, but apprenticeship has sustained livelihoods, built industries, and protected communities from economic helplessness.

Many of us were trained from adolescence to believe that a good life comes from earning a degree and getting a good job. For many people, that path is wise and stable. It can be strong insurance for the future. But not everyone will have the same access to higher education. In some countries, university is simply too expensive. In other cases, the need to earn a living early pushes people into professions that can generate income quickly.

In this chapter, we will look at apprenticeship from five angles to see how skills can be acquired, refined, and converted into value.

Apprenticeship by Chance

This is the kind of apprenticeship that happens when life places you in an environment you did not plan to exploit, yet the environment trains you anyway.

Consider Amber. Amber is a young graduate who moved from the suburbs to the city with the hope of landing a well paying job. But the reality of the city was not as romantic as it looked from a distance. Competition was intense. Graduates were everywhere. Opportunities were limited. Still, she stayed. She kept applying. She kept searching.

To survive, Amber took a job as a front desk clerk at a beauty salon. It was not part of her dream, but it was a way to pay bills while she waited for something better. As she worked, she began noticing the business behind the beauty. She watched customers come in and money go out. She noticed that the salon owner was doing well. Not only financially, but also socially. The owner had influence, confidence, and control over her schedule in a way Amber did not expect.

At first, Amber simply observed. Then she started assisting. She asked questions. She paid attention to technique, customer service, pricing, and daily operations. Without realizing it, she was being trained. What began as survival slowly became an education.

Over time, Amber's interest shifted. She began to see that her future did not have to look like the picture her community had drawn for her. She started thinking like a builder. She saved money. She practised. She improved. Eventually she began offering services outside work hours, building her confidence and her client base.

When her grandmother passed away and left a property for the grandchildren to sell and share, Amber used her share to open her own salon. Later she expanded and created a training centre for others who wanted to learn the skill.

Amber's story is fictional, but the pattern is real. Sometimes opportunity comes disguised as inconvenience. A flexible mind can discover a path inside an unplanned season.

A real world example that fits this idea is Tom Ford. He is widely known for fashion and fragrance, yet his first direction was architecture. During an internship for Chloe in Paris, he became drawn toward fashion. He returned to complete his academic programme, but he focused his energy on learning design. After graduation, he pursued fashion seriously and famously persisted until he secured an interview with designer Kathy Hardwick.

The lesson is simple. Places can reveal you to yourself. Sometimes you do not find gold in an environment, but you find the gold inside you.

Self-Taught Apprenticeship

Self taught apprenticeship happens when a person learns a skill without a formal trainer. The learner takes responsibility for the process, including practice, feedback, correction, and improvement.

This path can be powerful, but it is also risky. A mentor shortens your learning curve. A mentor corrects your blind spots early. Without guidance, you can spend months mastering the wrong thing or building habits that later become difficult to unlearn.

Still, self learning is more common today because information is accessible. With discipline, a person can learn valuable skills through online resources, observation, consistent practice, and deliberate refinement. Many professionals have built careers through this route, especially in creative and digital fields.

I also learned this personally when I entered the retail business of fashion and accessories without prior preparation. I did not have a manual. I learned by doing, failing, adjusting, and repeating. Over time, that experience taught me how business really works: customer psychology, inventory control, pricing, negotiation, and the discipline required to stay consistent. The biggest lesson was this: when nobody supervises you, your future depends on your self control.

However, self taught apprentices are vulnerable in industries where insiders exploit beginners. The music industry is a common example. Many artists have talent but lack knowledge of contracts, royalties, ownership, and negotiation. They focus on art, then lose the business. Talent may open the door, but knowledge protects you once you enter.

This is one reason some artists now prefer independence, aiming to maintain ownership of their work.

Kanye West is often mentioned as an example of self taught development. As a teenager, he was introduced to studio equipment by a friend, No ID, who later became a well known producer. That exposure pushed him deeper into music production. He practised, experimented, and sharpened his competence over time. Later, he worked as a producer at Rocafella Records before gaining wider attention as a rapper with Through the Wire.

His mother, Dr Donda West, was reportedly unhappy about his decision to leave school, and the broader point remains worth reflecting on: higher education can be a strong path, but not every career goal follows the same route.

This is not an argument against education. It is an argument against treating one path as the only path. There are also people like J Cole who completed a degree and still excelled in music. The deeper truth is that discipline can make different routes work, if the learner takes growth seriously.

In House Apprenticeship

In house apprenticeship is learning a skill within the family. A child learns a trade from a parent, an uncle, an older sibling, or a close relative. In many communities, this is how trades survive across generations. It is also how families protect themselves economically, because knowledge stays in the household and becomes a generational asset.

This method can be effective, but it comes with one major warning. If a person is forced into a family trade without interest, the learning may produce competence but not fulfilment. A skill can feed you, but resentment can drain you. That is why guidance must not become imprisonment.

Families should expose children to skills, but also allow room for personal choice and personal calling.

Talent Development Apprenticeship

Talent is a gift, but talent is not mastery. Mastery requires training.

Some people have obvious ability in music, art, writing, sport, design, public speaking, or leadership. They stand out early. But raw talent still needs structure, correction, repetition, and professional standards. Talent development apprenticeship is the process of placing that gifted person under a coach, teacher, or skilled professional who knows how to shape potential into consistent performance.

Many people fail not because they lack talent, but because they underestimate training. Talent without development often creates frustration. A person can have the gift and still remain stuck because they never built the habits that make the gift dependable.

A simple truth is this: talent can make you noticeable, but training makes you valuable.

Why Apprenticeship

There is a cultural lie that says the only respectable progress is academic progress. Formal education is important, and in many fields it is necessary. But many valuable skills are not fully taught in traditional schools. Trades like welding, carpentry, barbing, plumbing, tailoring, and masonry are often learned more effectively through apprenticeship.

Life also does not distribute opportunity equally. That is why apprenticeship remains a reliable way for individuals to build competence and earn a living through practical learning.

If you can combine formal education with apprenticeship, you create an advantage. If you cannot access university, apprenticeship can still provide dignity, income, and direction. The goal is not to impress society. The goal is to build a life that works.

The big question is how to choose.

Start with honesty. Consider your goals, your financial reality, your personality, your environment, and the type of future you want to build. When you make a choice based on reality and commit to disciplined learning, both routes can lead to a meaningful life.

Apprenticeship teaches a powerful lesson: education is not only what you know. Education is what you can do.

One option that combines the best of both worlds is a work study programme, especially at Master's level. In many countries, universities partner with companies so students can work while studying and earn both academic credit and professional experience. In France, this is popularly known as Alternance.

This model is especially common across parts of Western and Central Europe. France has built a strong national culture around Alternance, and similar work linked pathways are widely recognised in Germany, Austria, and Switzerland, where apprenticeship routes are deeply established and socially respected. The United Kingdom has also expanded its system through degree apprenticeships, including pathways that connect work and university level qualifications.

Outside Europe, the idea exists but is often structured differently. In Canada and the United States, it is frequently offered through university specific co op or work integrated learning programmes, and it tends to be more common in fields like engineering, business, computer science, and applied sciences. In many other regions, including parts of Africa, Latin America, and Asia, work experience during studies is often available through internships, placements, or informal arrangements, but it is less consistently standardized as a national degree linked apprenticeship pathway in the way Alternance is in France.

I highly recommend this route because it solves a common problem for graduates: having a degree but little real workplace experience. With Alternance, you build practical skills, learn professional standards, and develop a credible CV while still earning your qualification. By the time you graduate, you are not only certified. You are already experienced.

Closing thought

Apprenticeship is not a second-class path. It is a direct path into competence.

Degrees can open doors, but skill keeps you inside the room. Skills keep you paid when life is unpredictable. Skill gives you confidence because it is earned, not imagined.

So do not chase status at the expense of substance. Choose a path that builds you. If you are in school, use school well, but do not stop there. If you are outside school, do not see yourself as behind. Commit to learning, practise until you improve, and keep raising your standards.

In the human capital market, people do not reward your intentions. They reward your value.

Build value patiently, and your future will start responding to you.

EDUCATION BEYOND SCHOOL

When most people hear the word education, they immediately think of school. Classrooms. Timetables. Exams. Certificates. For many of us, modern education has become so closely linked to standardized assessment that we forget a simple truth.

Learning is bigger than school.

There are other productive ways of educating the human mind, and they deserve more attention. One of the most important is the holistic education movement, which promotes a broader view of what it means to be educated.

Holistic education began gaining prominence in the 1980s as a philosophy that encourages people to develop human values by connecting to their environment, their community, and their inner life. Instead of relying only on mainstream classroom routines, it emphasizes adaptive learning through experience, observation, and personal development.

A well known example of holistic education is the Montessori approach. Montessori education is built on a simple idea: the learning environment should help the learner become independent, focused, and capable of directing their own progress.

Government guided curricula have been the primary source of knowledge for generations. But the pace of modern life, technology, and global competition is forcing people to expand their learning beyond what schools can provide. To understand this idea clearly, it helps to look at two Latin roots that are often associated with education: educare and educere.

Educare: education as training

Educare means "to train." It refers to the process of grooming children from infancy by teaching them how the world works and how to use the resources around them.

This system has done a lot of good. It has built structure. It has increased literacy. It has improved discipline and created organized societies. But it also has a weakness.

Educare is largely instruction based.

A teacher passes down information, students memorize and practice it, and then a standardized test evaluates whether the student can reproduce the content. The problem is not that this method is useless. The problem is that it can become the only method, and when it becomes the only method, it can overlook a powerful human ability: the natural capacity to learn from within.

Learning is part of human nature. Nobody teaches a child how to desire understanding. The desire is already there. Even walking and speaking are acquired because the human being carries an instinct to learn and adapt.

Still, in many systems, formal education becomes narrow. People are pushed to learn content they do not care about, and sometimes education is used to reinforce social agendas, prejudice, and segregation. When education becomes a tool for control, it stops being liberation and becomes manipulation.

Another consequence is the artificial gap created between formal education and vocational education. If education is truly about training, then training should not be ranked by status. A society needs both academic thinkers and practical builders.

This is why education must expand.

Just because you are studying accounting does not mean you cannot explore psychology to understand human behavior. It does not mean you cannot study history to broaden your perspective. It does not mean you cannot learn communication skills to become more effective in the workplace.

If you want maximum results in life, you must learn to look beyond the four walls of the classroom.

Educere: education as drawing out

Educere means "to draw out" or "to lead out." This approach focuses on bringing out what is already within a person.

Many of us were trained to believe that enlightenment is only an outside to inside process. We learn something external, store it, then repeat it when needed. But humans also have another capacity.

We can generate new ideas.

We can create concepts that are not simply recycled information. This is how innovation happens. Many technological breakthroughs were born from imagination, intuition, and creative insight, not only from formal schooling.

Educere has been neglected in many school systems because it is harder to standardize. Yet it survives through cultural and spiritual practices like meditation, mindfulness, solitude, and reflection. These practices create a quiet environment where the mind can produce clarity without constant external noise.

Imagine a classroom where students begin the day by closing their eyes, breathing slowly, and calming their thoughts for a few minutes. That single practice could shift the atmosphere. It could reduce anxiety, improve attention, and make learning feel less tense.

The point is not to replace educare with educere. The point is to balance them.

Many great minds appear to have used both. They studied deeply, but they also relied on imagination and inner discovery. Educare strengthens discipline and builds knowledge. Educere strengthens intuition and fuels originality. When a person balances both, learning becomes more powerful and more personal.

The role of parents and early conditioning

Schools are not the only reason educere is neglected. Parents and guardians also play a role.

Some parents, with good intentions, train children to chase only one definition of success. They may suppress a child's natural interests and instincts, believing they are protecting them. But when a child's inner direction is repeatedly ignored, the adult version of that child can grow into frustration.

Think about the example raised earlier with Kanye West and his mother. Imagine if she had been strict to the point of threatening disownment if he chose music. Many parents have done similar things. The result is that many adults never discover their true potential, not because they are not gifted, but because what was inside them was never allowed to come out.

Educere is not just a learning method. It is also a permission structure.

It tells a person: there is something in you worth leading out.

Intuition: knowledge without conscious reasoning

Intuition is often defined as the ability to know something without prior reasoning or proof. That sounds strange because wisdom is usually described as sound judgment built from experience. Yet intuition still matters, because it often moves faster than conscious processing.

The conscious mind needs time. Intuition can feel immediate.

It is the inner signal that says something is off, even before you can explain why. It is the quiet pull toward an idea before the evidence appears. It is the inner direction that pushes some people into breakthroughs.

Human perception is limited. We cannot see everything around us. We cannot sense every force that exists. Yet through learning, experimentation, and insight, humanity has repeatedly discovered invisible systems and found ways to interact with them. What we call progress often begins as a thought that was not yet proven.

This is why relying only on external knowledge can limit a person. Sometimes the information within you can be more valuable than you expect.

The brain, learning, and a modern correction

Some motivational speakers still promote the old idea that people are either right brained or left brained, as if one side dominates the person. Modern research does not support the popular version of that claim. While the brain has specialized regions and hemispheric tendencies, it functions as an integrated unit. Both sides work together.

This matters because it protects you from false labeling.

You do not have to decide you are the creative type or the logical type as if you cannot develop the other side. Human beings are adaptable. Learning is flexible. Growth is possible.

Innate learning and the proof in early life

Even in newborns, we see signs of inborn learning processes. Babies do not receive lectures on how to self soothe, yet many begin sucking their fingers very early. Some sources describe this as a natural reflex. The key word is natural. Innate. Inborn.

If something is innate, it comes from inside.

You can call it intuition, instinct, reflex, inner intelligence, or any name that fits your belief system. The label matters less than the reality. There is an internal source of learning, and educere is the practice of creating conditions that allow it to come forward.

Teaching as ignition, not only instruction

Teaching should not be streamlined to educare only. A teacher should also be able to lead out what is already within the learner.

A strong teacher does not only transfer information. A strong teacher ignites something. They create an environment where curiosity becomes energy, and that energy becomes growth.

When inner energy is not guided well, it can turn into negative emotion. Envy, bitterness, greed, and resentment often grow in people who never learned how to transform pressure into purpose. Holistic education is not only academic. It is emotional. It is social. It is human.

Education is beyond school.

If you want to grow in life, you must explore all avenues of learning, including the learning that begins inside you. There is something within you that is stronger than your conscious mind's noise. I choose to call it intuition, and when it is trained with discipline and supported by knowledge, it can become one of your greatest assets.

Closing thought

School can train you, but it cannot complete you.

If you want real development, combine both worlds. Learn from teachers and books, and also learn from reflection, experience, and inner awareness. The more you expand how you learn, the more you expand what you can become.

SELF INVESTMENT

It is never a waste of time or money to invest in yourself, no matter the source. Real wealth begins inward and then shows itself outward, including in the quality of the people you attract and the opportunities you can handle.

In the human capital market, your skills are an asset. But an asset that cannot be seen is rarely chosen. In a supermarket, people reach for the product they notice first. In the job market, decision makers notice the professional who stands out through competence, confidence, and proof of value.

You trained to become a manager. Fine. What sets you apart from the millions of managers out there? What is your strongest advantage as a manager? And what have you done to grow that advantage?

That difference is your visibility.

Visibility

From 2014 to 2017, Coca Cola reportedly spent billions of dollars on advertising. Why would a global giant spend so much on publicity when the world already knows the brand? Because visibility must be maintained. In competitive markets, even the strongest brands fight to stay present in the public mind.

The same principle applies to you as a professional.

I have not[22]iced something while teaching at university. Some students perform well in tests and assignments, but they avoid speaking during interactive sessions. After class, I ask them why. Many say they do not want to impress others, or they do not like being the center of attention.

I understand that mindset because I used to behave the same way. But there is a problem. What you practise repeatedly becomes habit. And habits do not disappear automatically when you graduate.

A student who develops the habit of silence in class often becomes the employee who stays silent in meetings. The professional who stays silent in meetings becomes the professional who is overlooked for leadership. Not because they are not competent, but because their competence never becomes visible.

Now imagine your future.

You are in a meeting room with executives. Everyone is brainstorming. Ideas are flying. Strategies are being tested. Are you going to keep quiet because you do not want attention? Are you going to watch opportunities pass because you are trying to look modest?

Your classroom is training ground. It is a safe space to practise formal communication. Mistakes are normal there. Use your teacher as your sounding board. Ask questions. Speak. Contribute. Do not be too cool for school.

Visibility does not start after graduation. It starts while you are still preparing.

Continuing Professional Development

Many professionals stop learning once they meet what they consider the minimum requirement for a job. They become comfortable with a stable income and stop upgrading their competence. That comfort can feel harmless, but it often leads to stagnation.

The world is changing constantly, and technology increasingly dictates professional standards. New tools, new systems, and new expectations emerge every year. If you refuse to adapt, you risk becoming redundant.

Continuing Professional Development, often called CPD, is the habit of improving your competence through training, learning, and exposure. It can mean formal certification. It can also mean reading reliable articles, studying industry updates, watching professional lectures, attending workshops, and learning new software that improves your performance.

CPD is not only for people who want promotions. It is also for people who want protection. When companies downsize, outsource, or automate roles, the employee with outdated skills becomes the easiest to replace.

Many serious companies invest in their staff through workshops and training because they understand that human capital is not optional. A company that develops its people builds capacity, stability, and competitive advantage. The same logic applies to individuals. The more you invest in yourself, the more valuable you become.

Skills

The fear of failure and the fear of the unknown have pushed many people away from their potential. Some people fear change so much that they treat growth like an enemy. They stay in a comfort zone for years, repeating the same routine, and calling it stability.

One common reason for this is how we were trained to view learning. Many of us believe learning must only happen through a classroom curriculum. So we ignore the simplest paths to skill acquisition.

Reading is one of the most powerful traditional methods of learning. Through reading, you can discover a new skill. Through practice, you can develop it. Once you master a skill, you can trade it for value. The better your craft, the higher the price you can place on it.

From my experience working with a training and leadership company that helped professionals transition careers and climb in corporate environments, I noticed a pattern. Many people stop developing once they land a good job. They work for years without learning anything new. Then reality hits. Downsizing. Outsourcing. Automation. Sometimes software replaces what a person does. Sometimes robots take over tasks that were once human.

Sadly, this is when many decide to retrain themselves. But the smarter move is to develop before you are forced to.

If your skills are no longer needed, you become irrelevant in your field. And irrelevance can turn into job loss.

Sometimes life also forces good people to settle for less than they believe they deserve. A person with an MBA might accept a low paying role simply to survive while searching for better opportunities. That can be understandable.

But do not turn temporary survival into permanent settling.

If your skill has value, ask yourself an honest question. How much value do you place on your own competence? Many people blame employers for low pay, but sometimes the deeper issue is that the person never built enough leverage through specialization, proof, and excellence.

Specialized skills make you harder to ignore. When you know your value and you have evidence of it, you can confidently reject offers that do not reflect your worth, except when survival leaves no choice. Even then, keep your standards alive. Know when to climb higher. If your skill is truly precious, the right market will eventually respond.

Your Resources

One of my favourite brands is Hugo Boss, so I researched the story behind it. Hugo Ferdinand Boss was a German designer who began with workwear and uniforms. But what stands out in this story is how the next generation transformed that foundation into a global brand.

His grandsons, Uwe and Jochen Holy, did not simply inherit a business and hope it would grow. They acquired the skills needed to build it. One studied business, the other studied economics. That combination helped them expand the company into one of Germany's most successful fashion brands.

The message is clear. Training creates mental discipline. That discipline is a resource. With it, you can transform simple materials into products and opportunities. Plastic can become containers. Paper can become books. Bricks can become buildings. A uniform factory can become an empire.

When you put your skills to maximum use, quality becomes your signature. And people pay for quality.

From my own experience as a former retail store owner, I can tell you that some customers only buy the best they can find. Others buy what they can afford in the moment. Over time, those choices become habits.

The same is true for companies. Many businesses collapse because they focus only on financial returns and neglect human capital. A company that trains its employees consistently builds a workforce that becomes a valuable asset.

If you only buy quality shoes, you eventually own a quality collection. If a company consistently invests in high level training, it eventually builds a team of high level professionals.

Your Raw Material

What is your skill made of?

Is it natural talent or acquired competence? How much time have you invested in upgrading it? What is the thing within or around you that you can transform into a valuable commodity?

For some people, the raw material is a family business. For others, it is an artistic gift. But having raw material is not the same as having value.

A diamond has no market value while hidden under the earth. It becomes valuable when it is discovered, refined, cut, and presented in the right market. In the wrong environment, a diamond can be traded for something painfully small because the buyer does not understand its value.

That is a serious lesson for professionals.

Refine your raw material. Improve your skill to exceptional quality. Target the right market that appreciates it. Poor training produces poor results. Mediocre learning creates average professionals. What you put in is what you get out.

Your raw material needs discipline, education, and practice. It can be formal education, apprenticeship, direct experience, or a mixture of all three. The key is consistent growth.

Some countries even recognize working hours as a form of training in specific professions. For example, in parts of the United States, certain pathways allow legal apprenticeships that can lead to professional qualification under strict conditions. While this route is not common everywhere, it highlights a broader truth. Experience is a form of learning when it is structured, supervised, and intentional.

Time Invested

Time is not only a measure of age. It is a form of investment.

It is admirable to complete your education early and earn a respected qualification. But qualification is not the same as professionalism. Professionalism is knowledge plus experience. In many fields, experience is the missing ingredient that turns a graduate into a professional.

Many of the people who shape world affairs spend more time learning than the average person. Leaders in science, technology, education, and business often read, study, and build knowledge consistently. That commitment to learning is not a hobby. It is a strategy.

Nikola Tesla is a strong example of how time invested in study can shape a life. His brilliance was not only a gift. It was also the result of relentless curiosity and learning. He reportedly spent long periods reading and studying, even during difficult seasons of his life. Whether you are a genius or not, the principle still stands. Growth takes time, and purpose often takes time to discover.

There is no time too great to dedicate to self enlightenment. Once you identify your raw material, the next step is to harness it. Someone somewhere needs what you can offer. The first connection between seller and buyer may feel difficult, but once it is established, the quality of your work determines whether the buyer becomes a loyal customer.

Some professions require years of training to achieve excellence. Surgeons are not born with surgical skill. They become skilled through years of study and supervised practice. A doctor becomes a specialist through additional years of training. In the commercial world, this is the same logic that apprenticeship follows. Learn. Practise. Refine. Prove competence. Earn trust.

Closing thought

Self investment is not motivation. It is strategy.

If you want to rise in the human capital market, treat your growth like a serious project. Build visibility through competence. Keep learning through professional development. Evaluate yourself honestly through planning tools. Refine your raw material. Invest time until your skill becomes undeniable.

When you improve what is inside you, you change what the world can offer you.

THE INVISIBLE ENEMY

When I first discovered Steven Pressfield's *The War of Art* in my twenties, it shook something awake in me. It gave language to a struggle I had felt for years but could not fully explain. It helped me see something important about human nature and the quiet laws that shape progress. If there is one idea from that book that speaks directly to the struggles people face in building their lives and careers, it is this word: **Resistance**.

Resistance is the invisible enemy that shows up whenever you try to rise above your current condition. It is the force that makes growth feel heavy. It is that strange burden in the morning that makes you want to stay in bed even when you know you have work to do. It is the impulse that keeps you scrolling on your phone, watching television, or wasting hours on small comforts while the things that truly matter wait in silence.

Many people mistake this for laziness or a lack of talent. But it is deeper than that. Resistance is a universal human struggle. The mind naturally prefers what is familiar. It clings to what it already knows, even when that familiar place is keeping you small. Growth asks something from you. It asks effort, discipline, discomfort, and change. Resistance answers by whispering that comfort is safer than effort, that delay is harmless, and that you can always begin tomorrow.

But tomorrow is where many dreams go to die.

When you keep yielding to Resistance, you slowly begin to make peace with a lower version of yourself. You procrastinate. You avoid challenge. You settle into routines that feel safe but quietly rob you of your future. You begin to call stagnation stability. You fear change so deeply that growth starts to feel like a threat rather than a gift.

This is how many people remain trapped for years. Not because they are incapable, but because they have made an unspoken agreement with comfort.

And today, distraction has made this battle even harder. Your phone, your entertainment, your endless stream of noise can feed Resistance every single day. Distraction is not harmless. It is costly. Growth requires repetition. Learning requires attention. The brain builds strength through practice and consistency. When you keep interrupting your effort with distraction, you deny your mind the repetition it needs to grow. You remain stuck in the beginner stage, not because you cannot improve, but because you never stay with the work long enough.

Resistance also wears more dangerous masks. It appears not only as laziness, but also as ego, anger, pride, and self sabotage. When your inner energy is not directed toward meaningful work, it often turns inward and becomes bitterness, envy, or resentment. A person who is not building may begin criticizing. A person who is not progressing may begin blaming. A person who is not mastering themselves may begin wounding others.

In professional life, this can be disastrous. Resistance can use ambition itself against you. It can make you harsh, impatient, reactive, and destructive in the name of strength. It can tempt you to speak carelessly when angry, to burn bridges, to let pride damage relationships that wisdom should have protected. But real strength is not found in emotional reaction. Real strength is self control. Choosing your words carefully when you are upset is not weakness. It is mastery.

So what, then, is the antidote?

You do not defeat Resistance by waiting to feel inspired. You do not defeat it by negotiating with your moods. You do not defeat it by hoping one day you will suddenly feel ready. You defeat it through structure, clarity, and execution.

A clear goal is not just a productivity tool. It is training for the mind. It teaches you to direct your energy instead of leaking it. It teaches you to delay comfort for progress. It teaches you to move even when you do not feel like moving. Every time you honor a meaningful goal, you are training your mind to stop serving fear and start serving purpose.

That is one of the great lessons of adulthood. You must stop waiting for life to become easy before you become disciplined. Discipline is often what makes life easier.

If you want to change your professional life, your habits, or your future, you must first recognize this invisible enemy for what it is. Resistance wants to keep you in survival mode. It wants you to spend your life merely working, reacting, and enduring, without ever rising into your full potential. It wants you busy, distracted, emotionally ruled, and spiritually asleep.

Do not give it that victory.

Stand up. Choose the hard path on purpose. Train your mind. Guard your attention. Master your moods. And do the work that your better future is asking from you.

Because the life you want will not be built by comfort. It will be built by the quiet decision to move forward, even when Resistance tells you not to.

HUMAN CAPITAL

In today's economy, your value is not only your certificate. Your value is your **career capital**. The rare combination of skills, credibility, relationships, and results that makes you useful in any serious environment.

Human capital is the knowledge, abilities, and professional behaviors you can convert into outcomes. It includes technical skill, communication, emotional control, judgment, reliability, and your ability to learn fast. In practical terms, it is what you can deliver, how consistently you deliver it, and how easily others can trust you with responsibility.

Money matters, but money is not the engine. People are the engine. Organizations run on human capability. Nations grow when they develop people who can build systems, solve problems, innovate, and execute.

That is why countries that invest in education, training, and workforce development usually become stronger economically. Skills create independence. Skills reduce dependency. Skills attract investment. Skills turn resources into results.

From qualifications to proof

A degree can open doors, but the modern market rewards **proof**. Proof is your portfolio, your projects, your outcomes, your ability to explain what you did, and your reputation for getting things done.

This is why some graduates feel shocked after school. They expected the certificate to do the work for them. But hiring managers often think in three questions:

Can you do the job?
Can we trust you?
Can you work with people?

When you treat your development as a long term strategy, you stop chasing status and start building capability. You stop waiting for opportunity and start creating evidence.

Awareness as a competitive advantage

A modern professional must develop awareness, not only information. Awareness means you can think critically, separate facts from noise, and avoid being controlled by propaganda, trends, or group pressure. It also means you know how to learn, how to update yourself, and how to admit what you do not yet know.

In many fields, the biggest gap is not intelligence. It is judgment. People collect knowledge, but they do not develop discernment.

It is not too late

If you feel behind, remember this. Professional growth is not only a young person's game. Many people reinvent themselves in their thirties, forties, and beyond. Sometimes ambition pushes you early. Later, fulfillment becomes the stronger reason.

Your timeline is not the enemy. Your lack of direction is the enemy.

The deeper engine behind decision making

There is also a quiet psychological truth. Your mind keeps processing even when you are not consciously working. That is why people say "sleep over it." Clarity often comes when your nervous system is calm. A strong professional learns how to think strategically, regulate emotions, and make decisions without panic.

Treat your life like an enterprise. Protect your energy. Set priorities. Build routines. Invest in skill. Build evidence. Then the market responds differently.

Closing thought

Human capital is not an idea. It is leverage.

When you build career capital, you stop begging for value. You start negotiating from value.

WORKPLACE DYNAMICS

Many graduates enter the workplace with one major misunderstanding. They assume the office is like school. Do your work, be polite, and everything will be fair.

Work is not always fair. Work is a system.

People have incentives. People have insecurities. People have politics. People have egos. Some teams are healthy. Some teams are tense. Your job is to succeed without losing yourself.

This is not paranoia. It is professional realism.

Psychological safety and professional boundaries

In strong workplaces, psychological safety exists. People can speak up, ask questions, and admit mistakes without fear of humiliation. In weaker workplaces, people hide errors and play politics because fear runs the system.

You cannot control the culture, but you can control your boundaries.

Keep your personal life private. Do not overshare. Watch patterns before you trust. Be friendly, but do not confuse friendliness with loyalty. Some people collect information as a weapon, not as a connection.

The most common sources of tension

A lot of workplace conflict comes from predictable triggers:

Status competition
Insecurity and comparison
Poor communication
Micromanagement
Unclear expectations
Credit stealing
Passive aggression

Sometimes you will also meet the colleague who is not openly hostile but quietly undermines you. They delay your tasks. They distort your words. They "forget" important details. They exaggerate your mistakes.

In those moments, your best protection is not emotion. Your best protection is professionalism.

Document important work. Confirm decisions in writing. Clarify expectations early. Communicate calmly. Keep receipts.

How to handle difficult colleagues without burning out

Use a strategy, not a reaction.

Stay respectful, but be firm.
Do not argue in public.
Do not fight rumors with drama.
Escalate when necessary, with evidence.
Focus on outcomes, not ego.

If you are naturally calm, remember that calm can be misread as weakness. Practice assertiveness. If you are naturally confrontational, practice restraint. If you are sensitive, practice emotional regulation. Do not let people walk over you, bark when you must, hold your tongue when you need to, and learn to choose your battles wisely. You will make mistakes; you are human, but you will become more discerning over time.

The workplace does not only reward talent. It rewards emotional management. By the way, when you have to,

Closing thought

You cannot control people's insecurity, but you can control your professionalism.

Let your competence speak, let your boundaries protect you, and let your calm strategy keep you employed.

MENTORSHIP AND SPONSORSHIP

Mentorship matters, but modern career growth also requires something people rarely explain.

You need mentors, and you also need sponsors.

A mentor gives you advice, clarity, and correction. A sponsor uses their influence to open doors, recommend you, and place your name in rooms you cannot access alone.

Both are valuable, but they are not the same.

Mentors, coaches, and communities

Mentorship can come from three modern sources:

Mentors who guide your thinking and decisions
Coaches who improve a specific skill through feedback and practice
Communities of practice where you learn through peers, projects, and shared standards

Books can also mentor you, but relationships accelerate learning because feedback is real time.

How to choose the right guide

Do not choose mentors based only on charisma. Choose based on integrity, competence, and alignment. If someone is ego driven, manipulative, or jealous, distance is wisdom.

Also understand this. Mentorship is earned. Most mentors invest more when they see seriousness, humility, and consistency.

Show up prepared. Ask good questions. Apply feedback. Build trust.

Becoming a mentor yourself

Mentorship is not controlled by age. It is controlled by experience and clarity. The moment you have learned something valuable, you can teach someone behind you. Teaching is also a way to strengthen your own mastery.

Closing thought

Your career will not grow by talent alone. It grows by skill, proof, relationships, and visibility.

Find mentors who shape you. Find sponsors who advocate for you. Then become the kind of professional others trust to recommend.

GOALS

This chapter was inspired by a question I once asked a classroom full of second year university students: Where do you see yourself in ten years?

I expected big visions. I expected curiosity. I expected at least a few people to take me on a flight into their future. But only a handful had a clear answer. Most of the class had one plan only: graduate, then get a good job.

A job is important, but a job is not a life plan. A job is often a necessity. It pays bills. It gives structure. It can create stability. But without a bigger direction, many people end up floating through routines, accepting whatever life throws at them, not because the options are great, but because they never created alternatives.

There is nothing wrong with serving someone before you become the master of your own dream. In fact, it is often wise. Work experience can teach you what school cannot. It can build maturity, professional standards, and confidence. The problem begins when you stop there. When the only plan is survival, you become easy to control by circumstances, by people, and by fear.

Goals keep you in the driver's seat.

The modern purpose of goals

Many people think goals are only motivational quotes on social media. In reality, goals are a professional tool. They help you create focus, measure progress, and protect your time from distractions.

In modern professional life, goals do four things.

They give you direction.
They create discipline through structure.
They reduce procrastination by clarifying next steps.
They build confidence because you can see progress.

Without goals, you can be busy and still be stuck. You can work hard and still move in circles.

A smart goal is not only salary

Getting a job is not a goal. It is often a requirement of adulthood.

A smarter goal is to get a job that supports your bigger purpose. A job that helps you develop a skill, build a network, create credibility, and move toward something meaningful. Salary matters, but salary alone is not a vision. If money is the only reason you choose a path, you may end up in a role that pays you and drains you at the same time.

Ask yourself honestly.

Do I want this path because it fits me, or because it impresses people.

Am I choosing this role because I love the work, or because I love the image.
Will this job develop me, or will it only consume me.

If you are an artist by nature but you force yourself into a field only for prestige, you may earn income and still feel empty. That emptiness is not weakness. It is a signal that you are building a life that does not belong to you.

Goals are allowed to evolve

Some people avoid goal setting because they fear being wrong. They fear changing direction. They fear commitment. But goals are not a prison. Goals are a compass.

You can reset goals.
You can adjust goals.
You can abandon goals.

The key is that you do it intentionally, not emotionally. You change direction because you learned something new, not because you got tired or distracted. Mature professionals review their goals the way companies review strategy. They adapt when reality changes, but they do not drift.

Goals expand the mind

When you set a challenging goal, your mind starts stretching to meet it. You begin to ask better questions.

You begin to search for information. You begin to notice resources. You begin to see possibilities.

This is one reason goal setting feels uncomfortable at first. The mind prefers what it already knows. Goals demand growth, and growth demands effort.

If you feed your mind with useful information, your thinking improves. If you give your mind nothing to work with, you should not be surprised when it gives you nothing to build with. In the workplace, the people who grow fast are usually the people who keep learning. They keep updating. They keep improving how they think.

Self-actualization and the human need for meaning

Psychologist Abraham Maslow described self-actualization as the drive toward fulfillment, the desire to become what you are capable of becoming. You do not have to agree with every theory to understand the point. Humans suffer when they ignore their potential for too long. You can feel it in your mood. You can see it in your motivation. You can hear it in the way you talk about life.

When people use their strengths, they feel more alive. When they never use them, they often become bitter, bored, or emotionally exhausted.

This is why goals matter. A good goal is not just an achievement. It is a path toward becoming.

Here is a modern way to translate Maslow into practical direction. A meaningful goal usually has at least one of these elements:

Mastery, you get better at something real.
Contribution, your work helps others.
Alignment, your path feels like you.
Growth, you are challenged but not destroyed.

A simple goal framework you can actually use

To make goals practical, use three levels.

Vision
What kind of professional and human being do I want to become.

Strategy
What skills, credentials, and experiences will take me there.

Execution
What will I do this week and this month.

If you want it even simpler, use the professional version of SMART:

Specific
Measurable
Achievable
Relevant
Time bound

Then add one extra professional filter: evidence.

What proof will show that I am moving forward. Portfolio, project, certification, performance review, reference, results.

Goals become powerful when they become visible.

Closing thought

Goals are not for perfect people. Goals are for serious people.

If you do not design your future, you will live inside someone else's design, an employer's priorities, a friend's influence, or society's expectations. Set goals that build you, not goals that only impress people.

A job can pay you. A goal can transform you.

THE HARD WORK

Most modern workers are trained, often without realizing it, to accept one life script.

Get a job. Work for decades. Retire. Collect a pension. Hope the numbers are enough.

For many people, that script feels normal. It even feels responsible. A stable job, a mortgage, children in decent schools, a yearly vacation, and a routine that repeats from Monday to Friday. Some people are genuinely satisfied with that life, and there is nothing wrong with choosing stability.

The problem is not stability.

The problem is sleepwalking.

In this century, it is still common to see people spend an entire lifetime doing the same job without meaningful growth, without mobility, and without building anything that belongs to them. Think about the woman who remains a cleaner from her early twenties to her mid fifties. Think about the man who stays a security guard for thirty years. In many cases, they did not choose limitations because they were weak. They learned limitation. They inherited it from their environment. They were trained to survive, not to develop. Others know they want more but stay trapped because fear feels safer than effort.

But there are also people who cannot accept that pattern as the final definition of life. They want more than long service. They want more than building other people's dreams for forty years and retiring at the mercy of a pension system or a company package.

This is where an important distinction changes everything.

Working hard versus doing the hard work

Working hard usually means continuous labour for survival. It is the long routine of showing up, paying bills, and repeating the same cycle for decades. It often has no clear finish line except retirement.

Doing the hard work is different. Doing the hard work is focused effort with an end point. It is what you do to achieve a specific goal within a time frame.

Working hard is a lifestyle of labour.
Doing the hard work is a mission with completion.

This difference matters because working hard can keep you busy for life without making you feel fulfilled. Doing the hard work, even when it is difficult, often produces growth, freedom, and a sense of achievement because it leads somewhere.

So the real question is simple.

Do you want to spectate, or do you want to achieve.

If you want to achieve anything worth having, you must do the hard work.

Why hard work should have a finish line

Look around society and you will see the footprints of people who built wealth, influence, and legacy. They were not people whose goal was to work hard forever. They were people who did the hard work of building something, refining a skill, creating an asset, or achieving a target.

Hard work should end, because hard work is connected to goals.

You set a worthwhile goal.
You plan.
You execute.
You complete.

That is the rhythm.

The person who wants to own a small business must do the hard work of setting it up. Once the business is stable, the work changes. Systems replace struggle. Teams replace exhaustion. The business begins to produce income without demanding the same level of physical stress.

That is not laziness. That is leverage.

I lived this experience in a retail business. The setup was not magic. It required planning, patience, and action. It took time to move from idea to plan, and from plan to execution. But once the business was in motion, it became a more efficient way to generate income. The hard work had an end point, and after that, the business could run with the help of other competent people.

This pattern is not rare. It happens every day. The difference is not luck. The difference is that someone was willing to do the hard work before the reward appeared.

Hard work appears in every field

Hard work does not belong only to entrepreneurship. It belongs to every serious achievement.

The athlete who wants to win must do the hard work of training.
The student who wants to pass must do the hard work of studying.
The writer who wants to publish must do the hard work of writing consistently.
The scientist who wants discovery must do the hard work of research.
The entertainer who wants excellence must do the hard work of practice.

The shared principle is this. When the goal is achieved, that phase of hard work ends. A new phase begins, often with higher standards, but not the same kind of struggle.

Working hard is different. Working hard often ends only when age, exhaustion, or years of service force retirement.

Do not sacrifice your whole life to survival

Working nine or ten hours daily for years can slowly steal your life without asking permission. You miss family moments. You miss friendships. You miss quality time with yourself. You become so focused on earning that you forget to live.

I am not against work. I am for experience. A graduate should enter the job market, learn the system, and build professional maturity. But while you are gaining experience, you should also be pushing the envelope.

If you feel you deserve more than your current circumstances, it is not arrogance. It is a signal. You can change your condition by doing the hard work.

If you do not like your job, do the hard work of searching strategically for a better one.
If you do not like your position, do the hard work of upgrading your qualifications.
If you want to change your body, do the hard work of discipline in food and movement.
If you want to become an entrepreneur, do the hard work of building the business.

Change rarely begins with comfort. Change begins with effort.

Own your choices

The side of the fence you choose is your responsibility.

Do not blame your boss forever.
Do not blame society forever.
Do not blame your partner forever.

Sometimes people truly face unfair systems, and that is real. But even in difficult systems, the individual still has choices. The moment you accept that your life is your project, you stop waiting for rescue and start building options.

If you refuse to do the hard work, you will most likely work hard for most of your life.

The real reason passive income matters

When people hear passive income, they imagine flashy internet stories. But the real idea is simpler.

Build an asset that reduces the amount of labour your survival requires.

It does not have to be a multimillion business. It can be a small venture, a professional specialization, a high value skill, a product, a service, or a career ambition that gives you stability and freedom.

The point is not to escape work. The point is to escape endless struggle.

If you work extremely hard to earn a fixed salary and you settle there permanently, you may be accepting less than your potential. It can be a temporary stage, yes. But if it becomes your final stage, you may be underusing your most powerful resource: your mind.

Closing thought

Hard work is not punishment. It is the price of change.

Working hard is survival. Doing the hard work is transformation.

So choose a goal that is worth your effort. Create a plan. Execute with discipline. If you feel that desire to leap, do not let fear become your boss. You might fail, yes, but you might succeed. And success changes your whole relationship with life.

Do the hard work. Then let the results speak.

AFTERWORD

Forget the fear of whether your goal will work out or not. Do the work anyway.

One reason goal pursuit matters is not only the outcome. It is what the pursuit does to you while you are moving. When you commit to a goal and stay consistent, you build mental discipline. You train your attention. You train your patience. You train your ability to focus even when you do not feel motivated.

That is a form of strength many people never develop.

In this afterword, I want to touch on neuroscience lightly to explain a simple idea. Your brain changes when you learn. Your brain changes when you practise. Your brain changes when you focus.

Your brain is not fixed

For a long time, people believed the brain was mostly fixed after childhood, as if adulthood is a slow decline and nothing more. Today, we know the brain is more adaptable than that. Through neuroplasticity, your brain can form new connections and strengthen existing ones. When you repeatedly practise a skill, your brain becomes more efficient at that skill. With time, what felt difficult can begin to feel natural.

You do not need to be a scientist to understand the value of this.

When you learn a new ability, you are not only gaining knowledge. You are building new pathways. You are upgrading your system. That is why consistent practice feels like transformation. It is transformation.

Learning builds connections

Think about a skill like playing the piano, learning a new language, or mastering a digital tool for work. At the beginning, your mind feels slow. You make mistakes. You forget. You repeat. Then something changes. The repetition creates familiarity. The familiarity creates confidence. The confidence creates speed.

That change is not magic. It is your brain responding to stimulation.

This is also why distraction is expensive. When you never stay with anything long enough, you do not give your brain the repetition it needs to build strong connections. You remain in the beginner stage in many areas, not because you lack intelligence, but because you lack sustained focus.

Goals train your attention

A goal is not just a wish. A goal is a training structure for your mind.

When you set a goal and work toward it consistently, you are teaching your brain to concentrate on a target. You are also teaching yourself to delay comfort for progress. Over time, this builds a quiet confidence. You stop feeling helpless, because your mind starts trusting your ability to follow through.

This is why goal setting is not only professional. It is psychological.

It changes how you see yourself.

You already have proof

Look around you. Neuroplasticity is not only a scientific word. It is a human experience.

Most of us walk and talk every day as if it is automatic. But we had to learn to walk. We had to learn to talk. We did not become capable in one day. We became capable through repetition, correction, and time.

If you could learn those complex skills as a child, you can learn new skills as an adult.

Your age is not the limit. Your consistency is the limit.

A final encouragement

Be modest. Treat people fairly. Be kind and optimistic. These qualities do not make you weak. They make you steady. And steadiness matters in a world full of noise.

With time, you will discover that you are living in moments you once dreamed about. Even if you are not financially buoyant yet, you can still carry a strong inner confidence. The confidence that you are moving. The confidence that you are building. The confidence that you are not stuck forever.

Begin to observe life like a learner. Let your environment become a classroom. Let your experiences become lessons. Let your mistakes become feedback, not shame.

Your mind is capable of stretching farther than you think, but only if you pull the thread.

Start doing the things you dream of doing. It is not mainly a question of whether you can. It is a question of whether you will commit long enough to become the person who can.

www.ingramcontent.com/pod-product-compliance
Lightning Source LLC
LaVergne TN
LVHW050939080826
845145LV00004B/1328

* 9 7 8 0 9 9 3 5 2 3 7 5 5 *